MASSACRE IN MUNICH

HOW TERRORISTS CHANGED THE OLYMPICS AND THE WORLD

by Don Nardo

Content Adviser: Dennis Showalter, PhD
Professor of History
Colorado College

COMPASS POINT BOOKS
a capstone imprint

Compass Point Books are published by Capstone,
1710 Roe Crest Drive, North Mankato, Minnesota 56003
www.mycapstone.com

Editor: Catherine Neitge
Designers: Tracy Davies McCabe and Catherine Neitge
Media Researcher: Eric Gohl
Library Consultant: Kathleen Baxter
Production Specialist: Lori Barbeau

Image Credits
Alamy: Sueddeutsche Zeitung Photo, 41; AP Photo: 5, 8, 10, 11, 37, 52, dpa/picture-
alliance/Olympische Spiele, 46, Kurt Strumpf, cover, 13, 39, 51, 59 (top); Capstone:
24; Corbis: Bettmann, 33, 35; DVIC: NARA, 19; Getty Images: AFP/Stringer, 57
(bottom), Hulton Archive/Keystone, 20, 31, Joerg Koch, 29, Keystone-France, 43,
Mondadori, 36, Popperfoto/Rolls Press, 53, *Sports Illustrated*/Heinz Kluetmeier, 7;
Library of Congress: 15; Mary Evans Picture Library: Weimar Archive, 56; Newscom:
ABACA/PA Photos/Humphreys Owen, 58 (right), akg-images/Bildarchiv Pisarek, 16,
dpa/picture-alliance, 9, 25, 26, 44, 47, 48, 49, 55, EPA, 58 (left), Everett Collection,
18, 23, picture-alliance/Peter Kneffel, 45, ZUMA Press/Keystone Pictures USA, 17, 57
(top); Shutterstock: Iurii Osadchi, 59 (bottom)

Library of Congress Cataloging-in-Publication Data
Cataloging-in-publication information is on file with the Library of Congress.
ISBN 978-0-7565-5292-3 (library binding)
ISBN 978-0-7565-5296-1 (paperback)
ISBN 978-0-7565-5300-5 (ebook PDF)

Printed in the United States of America, in Stevens Point Wisconsin.
092015   009222WZS16

TABLEOFCONTENTS

ChapterOne
INTO THE WORLD'S AWARENESS

In the early morning of Tuesday, September 5, 1972, Will Grimsley awoke to what turned out to be the most important door-knock of his life. The veteran Associated Press (AP) sportswriter was sure no one would bother him at dawn unless something significant was happening.

As for what that something might be, Grimsley had no clue. The summer Olympic Games, held this time in Munich, West Germany, were a little more than half over. Dubbed the "cheerful Olympics" by the Germans, so far they had lived up to that hopeful bit of hype.

Dragging himself out of bed, Grimsley lumbered toward the door of his assigned quarters—Room 4B in the area set aside for journalists near Munich's Olympic Village. (The village was the fenced-in group of buildings where the athletes stayed.) Of the many AP reporters covering the games, Grimsley was the most experienced. Maybe one of his colleagues had a practical question of some kind. Perhaps it had to do with the best way to cover a specific athletic event. But why now? Couldn't it wait until after breakfast?

To Grimsley's surprise, he found that his visitor was not one of his AP co-workers. Instead the door opened to a messenger with a grim expression on his face. "Some Arabs have busted into the Israelis' quarters and are killing people," the man told Grimsley, who snapped fully

"Some Arabs have busted into the Israelis' quarters and are killing people."

West German sharpshooters worked their way up Olympic Village buildings in a futile attempt to confront Palestinian terrorists.

awake. "They've quarantined the village," the messenger went on. "The press and visitors are locked out."

As an experienced reporter, Grimsley was not worried about being locked out of a crime scene by police or security forces. He quickly dressed himself to look like an Olympic official. The disguise got him into both the Olympic Village and the temporary command center the police had set up inside the village. No one questioned him.

Like the proverbial fly on the wall, Grimsley was able to see what was happening. The West German police knew only that an unknown number of men were holding some of the Israeli athletes and coaches hostage. The details were still unclear.

Later that morning, future AP reporter Robert H. Reid was sitting with his wife in the stands of Munich's Olympic Park—the main stadium for the games. The American couple were living temporarily in Augsburg, a small city near Munich. Reid was stationed in West Germany while he finished his hitch in the U.S. Army.

For more than a year the couple had been looking forward to seeing the games from the best seats they could get. Now the time had come. It was a beautiful sunny morning—"clear blue sky, shorts and shirt-sleeve kind of weather," Reid later recalled. "The scene in Munich's Olympic Park on Sept. 5, 1972, was idyllic—except for a helicopter from the German border police circling over buildings of the nearby village where the athletes lived.

"If you shaded your eyes, squinted against the blinding sunlight and knew where to look, you could just make out the images of armed uniformed German police standing on the buildings. Turn away and the horror of what was unfolding seemed to disappear." The horror was that

A West German police officer stood guard as Olympic events continued during the hostage crisis.

eight Palestinian gunmen from the terrorist group Black September had slipped into the Olympic Village and seized Israeli athletes, coaches, and officials.

Despite the crisis in the Olympic Village, the athletic events in the stadium continued. Reid and his wife noted that Olympic officials did not yet feel compelled to postpone the long-planned sporting spectacle. "In an era before the Internet, before smartphones and before 24-hour news cycles," Reid later wrote, "there was little

tension in the air." The only indication of anything wrong, aside from the helicopter and the rooftop police, he said, was a one-word headline in a German newspaper: *Geiselnahme*, meaning "Hostage Taking."

In the late morning, several hundred yards closer to the crime scene, AP sports reporter Karol Stonger was eager to get inside the Olympic Village to cover the crisis. Local police had closed off the main entrances. However, like her colleague Will Grimsley, Stonger was highly resourceful. She borrowed a team jacket from an

INSIDE THE COMMAND POST

Police closed off the Olympic Village, but it didn't keep some reporters from getting in.

In his long career, Associated Press reporter Will Grimsley covered 15 Olympic Games, including the tragic 1972 games in Munich. When he found out what was happening in the Olympic Village, Grimsley realized he had loaned his press pass to another AP reporter. So he threw on a blue blazer and pinned on, in his words, "a souvenir pocket patch similar to those worn by officials—an eagle and five Olympic rings." Then he hurried to the village, hoping to find the command post set up by the West German police. The blazer and patch got him through the village's gate. Inside, he saw a black van parked in a roped-off area near the building where the Israeli athletes were being held. "This was the command post," he later recalled. "The Olympic patch which had gotten me through the gate of the secured Village permitted me to stride unchallenged inside the ropes—still mistaken as an official American observer."

Officials in the command post were communicating with Israeli Premier Golda Meir in Tel Aviv and West Germany's Chancellor Willy Brandt in Bonn. It was up to the Germans to negotiate with the hostage takers because Meir had sent word that the Israeli government would not: "We will not deal with terrorists."

Grimsley managed to quietly telephone the AP office at the Olympic press center with news of what was happening. Speaking in a whisper, he told the AP what was going on. But he had a problem, he later wrote: "I was the only newsman inside the ropes with access to world-shaking decisions—and it was useless. I didn't know a word of German."

A police officer blocked the gate to the Olympic Village as two Australian athletes tried to enter.

American swimmer and wet her hair to make it appear she'd recently been in the pool. In that clever disguise, she walked right past the guards.

Stonger climbed up onto the roof of a building that overlooked the Israeli team's apartments. From there she could see part way into the room where the hostages were being held. And the hostage takers could see her. For the next 12 hours she watched the drama unfold. She saw

A cameraman was thrown out of the Olympic Village after he tried to film the Israeli team's apartment building.

the kidnappers make their primary demand—an exchange of the Israeli hostages for some Palestinians held in Israeli prisons.

One of Stonger's AP associates, German photographer Kurt Strumpf, also tried to get inside the Olympic Village. But the German police had steadily tightened security in the area, and he was unable to do so. Still, he ended up taking the iconic photo of the crisis.

To line up the shot, Strumpf positioned himself on a building facing the Olympic Village. Several minutes went by. Then he saw movement on the balcony of the apartment where the hostages were being held. Peering through his telephoto lens, Strumpf saw a terrorist standing on the balcony. The unknown Palestinian's face was hidden by a ski mask.

Strumpf quickly snapped the camera's shutter and later found that he'd created an arresting, chilling image. To the viewer, the figure appeared to lack all traces of humanity. It was as if an alien being had appeared from some unknown place, a monstrous creature staring out over the balcony, searing its soulless image into the world's awareness.

Strumpf's photo did not just capture the hateful forces that had disrupted the games. It also was a powerful reflection of the evil in all terrorism. Yet as effective as this photo was, it was only one of dozens taken that day by talented photojournalists at the games. Together, they depict a riveting array of historical horror and human tragedy.

What neither Strumpf nor anyone else knew as the day unfolded was that the crisis would not end well. The "cheerful Olympics" would be known for the kidnapping and murder of 11 members of the Israeli Olympic team— the Munich massacre.

Strumpf's photo did not just capture the hateful forces that had disrupted the games. It also was a powerful reflection of the evil in all terrorism.

The photo of a masked Palestinian terrorist instantly brings to mind the horror of the 1972 hostage crisis at the Munich Olympics.

ChapterTwo
MAKING UP FOR THE PAST

West German officials began preparing for the 1972 Munich Summer Olympics in the late 1960s. In addition to the many administrative and construction problems encountered by all Olympic planners, they faced an especially thorny challenge. How could they distance themselves from the last games hosted by Germans?

The nation's first Olympic experience had occurred in 1936. Germany was then in the iron grip of dictator Adolf Hitler and his brutal Nazi regime. The 1936 Summer Games were held in Germany's capital, Berlin, from August 1 to 16. Nearly 4,000 athletes representing 49 countries took part. Germany fielded the largest single team with 348 athletes. The second-biggest team, numbering 312, was that of the United States.

The large size of the U.S. team was not the only thing about it that was considered noteworthy. Also significant was that 18 of its members were African-Americans. People across the world were eager to see how Hitler would react to this fact. After all, for years he and his Nazi followers had trumpeted to the world the alleged superiority of the German race. They had also emphasized the supposed inferiority of other races, including blacks.

As the date of the games approached, particularly worrisome for the Nazis was the lofty reputation of one of the black American athletes. Track and field competitor

Jesse Owens was the most successful athlete at the 1936 Olympics, winning four gold medals.

Jesse Owens had set three world records and tied another in a 1935 track meet. He was seen as the favorite to win several gold medals in Berlin. And if he did so, he would beat his supposedly superior German counterparts, embarrassing Hitler and his government.

Jews were also inferior in the eyes of Hitler and his Nazis. Since taking power in Germany in January 1933, the regime had followed an anti-Semitic policy. Jews

were regular victims of insults, beatings, and blatant discrimination. Germany's new anti-Semitic laws banned Jews from all professional jobs. They could no longer be doctors, teachers, judges, or lawyers. Growing numbers of Jews could not find jobs in the theater and the arts.

German Jews were steadily forced out of athletics. One of them, Gretel Bergmann, had set the German record for the high jump in 1931, before the Nazis had come to power. Once Hitler and the Nazis were in charge, she became a frequent target of bigotry. Only two weeks before the opening of the 1936 Berlin Games, the government cut her from Germany's Olympic team.

Gretel Bergmann won high jump titles in Germany, England, and the United States. The Nazis removed her name from German record books, and it was not restored until 2009. She turned 101 in 2015 and has lived in the United States since 1937.

Germans salute the Nazi flag during opening ceremonies of the 1936 Olympics.

But the Nazis' removal of Bergmann and most other Jewish athletes from the team took place quietly, behind the scenes. Other countries had threatened to boycott the games if German Jews were not allowed to compete. That would have greatly embarrassed Hitler. So he tried to sway world opinion in his favor—and prevent a boycott—by giving the impression that he and his government were not anti-Jewish. During the games they camouflaged their racism and anti-Semitism. Hitler ordered the removal of anti-Semitic graffiti from the streets and allowed fencer Helene Mayer, whose father was Jewish, to compete in the games. (She won second place, earning a silver medal.)

Following its invasion of Poland in 1939, the German army launched a campaign of terror. It is believed that at least 3 million Polish Jews and nearly 2 million non-Jewish Polish civilians were murdered.

The Nazis' disdain for and prejudice against blacks and Jews continued in the following years. After setting World War II in motion with Germany's invasion of Poland in 1939, Hitler also initiated a horrifying anti-Semitic scheme. It was intended to rid Europe of all

The bones of Jewish victims were still in crematoriums when World War II ended in 1945.

Jews through a highly organized system of mass murder. By the conflict's close in 1945, the Nazis had used machine guns, gas chambers, and starvation to slaughter more than 11 million people, including 6 million Jews, two-thirds of the Jewish population in Europe.

Hitler called this attempt to exterminate an entire people the "Final Solution." But the world came to know it as the Holocaust. A ghastly stain on Germany's reputation, it badly marred the nation's image for decades to come. The planners of the 1972 Munich Games hoped to erase

Security at the Olympics was deliberately light. Unarmed police officers wearing pastel blue safari-style uniforms and carrying walkie-talkies patrolled the grounds.

that stain and portray a new democratic and optimistic West Germany.

Postwar West German governments had long been eager to make amends to Jews both inside and outside of Germany. Most surviving Jews left Europe after the war. Many settled in Israel, the United States, Canada,

Australia, Great Britain, South America, or South Africa. In the early 1930s, 60 percent of all Jews lived in Europe. Five years after World War II, only 30 percent lived in Europe, and more than half lived in North America or South America.

West Germany began making restitution payments to Holocaust survivors in 1953. And in the 1960s the government banned anti-Semitic speech in public. These were only a few of the efforts of West Germany's leaders to make up for the hateful and inhumane anti-Jewish policies of the past. The leaders had high hopes for the Munich Olympics. In their eyes, having the Israeli team come to Germany and compete in a spirit of friendship would be a major step toward restoring the nation's long-damaged reputation.

But another kind of problem made itself felt at the games. Ever since its founding, the Jewish homeland—Israel—had been embroiled in a different kind of anti-Jewish hatred than that perpetrated by the Nazis. It was these bad feelings for Israel that disrupted the Munich Games.

When Munich hosted the Olympics in 1972, Israel had existed for only 24 years. In fact, until immediately after World War II, no Jewish homeland existed anywhere. Instead, Jews in various numbers lived in dozens of countries around the world. When Hitler came to power in 1933, for example, about 565,000 Jews lived in Germany, out of the county's overall population of 67 million.

When Munich hosted the Olympics in 1972, Israel had existed for only 24 years.

Because of the Nazis' anti-Semitic policies and actions, however, more than half of Germany's Jews had fled by the start of the war in 1939. Tens of thousands emigrated to Palestine, then overseen by the British. For them and many other Jews, Palestine was inviting from historical and cultural standpoints. As everyone knew, the region had been the site of the two ancient biblical Hebrew kingdoms—Israel and Judah.

Directly after the war, from 1945 to 1948, many more European Jews settled in Palestine. Most of them lived in large refugee camps run by the British and the newly formed United Nations (U.N.). So many Jews moved to the area that they increasingly came into conflict with local Arabs. For a while the British tried to work out a solution that would please both the Arabs and the Jews. But they soon found themselves the target of armed groups on both sides who demanded that they pull out of the region. Early in 1947 the British announced that they would leave Palestine the following year.

The U.N. formed the Special Committee on Palestine. The committee's goal was to study the situation and recommend the best way to broker peace between the Arabs and the Jews. The U.N. announced that when the British left in 1948, it would divide Palestine. There would be an independent Arab state and an independent Jewish state. In addition, the city of Jerusalem, sacred to both sides, would be administered by a group of international managers.

The Jews accepted the U.N. plan. But the Arabs did

An Israeli fighter dashed across two comrades who formed a human bridge over barbed wire. Jewish soldiers fought Arab troops unhappy with an independent Israel in 1948.

not, and fighting erupted between the two sides. Things came to a head on May 14, 1948, the day British control of the area ended. The Jews decided to ensure that the homeland the U.N. had promised would become a reality. They declared that Israel was an independent country. The next day five Arab nations attacked Israel. To the surprise of many, despite being badly outnumbered, Israel's soldiers defeated the attackers, and Israel survived its first year of existence. In June all sides accepted a U.N. ceasefire.

In the years that followed, tensions in the region remained high. Palestinian Arabs, along with other Arabs

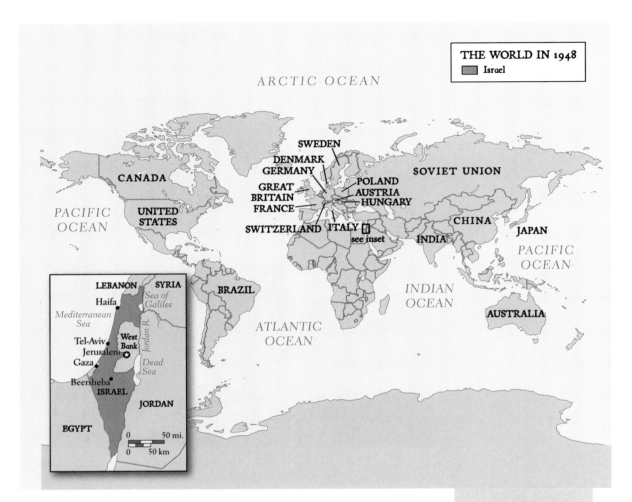

ARCTIC OCEAN

SWEDEN
DENMARK
GERMANY
CANADA
GREAT
BRITAIN
FRANCE
POLAND
AUSTRIA
HUNGARY
SOVIET UNION

PACIFIC
OCEAN
UNITED
STATES

SWITZERLAND ITALY
see inset
CHINA
JAPAN
INDIA

PACIFIC
OCEAN

BRAZIL

INDIAN
OCEAN

AUSTRALIA

ATLANTIC
OCEAN

LEBANON SYRIA
Haifa
Sea of
Galilee
Mediterranean
Sea
Tel-Aviv
Jerusalem
Gaza
West
Bank
Jordan R.
Dead
Sea
Beersheba
ISRAEL
JORDAN
EGYPT
0   50 mi.
0   50 km

and non-Arab Muslims in the Middle East, continued to oppose Israel. They argued that it was not a legitimate country and had no right to exist. But Israel, strongly backed by Great Britain and the United States, maintained itself as a small but militarily strong democracy.

Like other independent nations, Israel joined the United Nations and took part in global diplomacy. The Israelis also began competing in international athletic competitions, including the Olympic Games. Their first summer Olympic experience was in Helsinki, Finland,

Israel became an independent state and homeland for Jews in 1948.

DID GERMAN LEADERS KNOW IN ADVANCE?

The Munich massacre dominated newspaper coverage on September 6, 1972.

A 2012 cover story in Germany's leading news magazine, *Der Spiegel*, presented disturbing claims about the hostage crisis. There was evidence, it said, that West German officials had known in advance that members of a Palestinian group would stage an attack during the Olympics. *Der Spiegel* said there was also evidence that West German officials covered up their failure to stop the terrorists.

According to the magazine, a German embassy officer in Beirut, Lebanon, heard on August 14, 1972, that "an incident would be staged" by the Palestinians during the Olympic Games in Munich. A warning was sent to officials in West Germany with the recommendation that they "take all possible available security measures" against such an attack.

Der Spiegel said the warning was dismissed. The magazine also implied that German authorities failed to act on information reported in an Italian magazine. *Der Spiegel* reported that "three days ahead of the deadly hostage-taking, the Italian magazine *Gente* wrote that terrorists from Black September were planning a 'sensational act during the Olympic Games.'"

Der Spiegel also said documents show that "responsible officials seem to have attempted to erase any evidence of their failures to prevent the attack."

The Israeli delegation entered the Olympic Stadium during opening ceremonies. Days later 11 of its members would be dead.

in 1952, where its team numbered 26. The Israelis also participated in the Summer Games in Melbourne, Australia, in 1956; Rome, Italy, in 1960; Tokyo, Japan, in 1964; and Mexico City, Mexico, in 1968.

Israeli athletes next prepared for the 1972 Munich Olympics. When the team left for West Germany in early August of that year, it numbered 27 athletes. They had trained to compete in seven sports—track and field, fencing, sailing, swimming, shooting, weight lifting, and wrestling.

Athletes were not the only people who were getting ready for the Munich Games. All sorts of journalists, from writers and reporters to announcers and photographers, also made their preparations. Among them was Germany's veteran photojournalist Kurt Strumpf. He had joined the AP in 1957 in Frankfurt, and over the years he had taken many impressive photos. Some of them were of German news events, but he often covered important international events. Among them were the building of the Berlin Wall in 1961 and the Olympic Games of 1960, 1964, and 1968.

While on his way to Munich, with his cameras neatly stored in a large travel bag, Strumpf had no inkling that he would produce the iconic image of the games. Nor did AP sports reporter Karol Stonger imagine that she would end up on the roof of a building in an effort to tell the world about an unfolding crisis. The risk she would have to take didn't stop her. "You don't think about it," she said in a 1973 newspaper interview. "As a reporter, you do it instinctively. They say to go, and you go. It hits afterward. I never thought an Arab would shoot me, and he certainly could have."

One person who headed to Munich in August and later snapped images of the crisis was not yet a professional photographer. "A friend of mine was a track coach," recalled Bill Temko, then only 18 and a recent high school graduate. "He had a couple of his runners on the Olympic team," Temko said. "He had a deal to write some articles for *Ebony* and *Jet* [magazines]. And he asked me if I would go and take photos for the articles." The young man had no way of knowing he would be photographing terrorists.

The terrorists—eight Palestinian men not much older than Temko—also flew to Munich in August. They belonged to a group called Black September. The name came from an incident that had occurred in Jordan, Israel's eastern neighbor, in 1970. On September 16, Jordan's King Hussein started a major military action against Palestinian Arabs who had taken control of parts of his country. The king's troops killed several thousand Palestinians and expelled thousands more. Palestinians thereafter bitterly referred to the incident as "Black September."

A splinter group of the expelled Arabs took the name Black September. Its members had two initial goals—to take revenge on King Hussein and his country, and to undermine Israel. Black September achieved its first goal when it assassinated Jordan's prime minister, Wasfi al-Tel, in November 1971.

Then the group's leaders started planning a major action against Israel. They reasoned that most people would expect them to strike somewhere within the Jewish state itself. Instead they would do the unexpected and

Mountains loom in the distance behind Munich's Olympic Stadium.

hit the Israelis at an important international event. That would not only harm their sworn enemy, but it also would provide Black September with worldwide publicity. The Munich Olympics seemed like the perfect opportunity to accomplish both aims.

ChapterThree
THE MASSACRE

It was near dawn on Tuesday, September 5, 1972. In the Olympic Village, not far from the games' main stadium, the Israeli athletes were asleep. The night before, most had watched a performance of the popular musical *Fiddler on the Roof* in downtown Munich and had afterward gone out for dinner. Then they had returned to the five apartments assigned to them in the building at 31 Connollystrasse in the Olympic Village. All were in bed before midnight. The games were only about half over, and it was essential for them to be rested enough to compete well.

In the darkness on the far side of the perimeter fence closest to Connollystrasse, eight men quietly approached. They were wearing Olympic track suits and carrying duffel bags, but they were not athletes. They were members of the Palestinian terrorist group Black September. Instead of clothes, towels, and athletic equipment, their bags contained AK-47 assault rifles, ammunition, and grenades.

The eight terrorists quickly scaled the 7-foot (2-meter) chain-link barrier and were inside the Olympic Village within seconds. And they weren't alone. Several Canadian athletes were returning from a night of drinking. As they sneaked back to their dorm rooms, they helped the Palestinians scale the fence. Late-night partiers often hopped the fence rather than go through the official entrance.

> Instead of clothes, towels, and athletic equipment, their bags contained AK-47 assault rifles, ammunition, and grenades.

Members of the Israeli Olympic delegation visited Dachau on the eve of the Olympics. The Dachau concentration camp was the first built by the Nazis and is 10 miles (16 kilometers) from Munich.

Having made it past the outside fence, the terrorists walked through the village's streets casually, as if they were residents. This was part of the plan. If they happened to run into anyone along the way to Building 31, it was essential that they look like nothing more than late-returning athletes.

After saying good-bye to the unsuspecting Canadians, the Palestinian intruders went inside Building 31. They removed ski masks from their bags and pulled the masks over their heads. One of them took a stolen key from his pocket. Then they walked to the door of Apartment 1, where four Israeli coaches and three other members of the delegation were staying. One of the masked men tried the key. But the lock refused to turn, so he began fiddling with it.

Inside the apartment, wrestling referee Yossef Gutfreund suddenly awoke to a scratching noise. Forty years old and married, with two young daughters, Gutfreund had once been a wrestler in the heavyweight division. Physically speaking, he was a monster of a man, standing more than 6 feet (183 centimeters) tall and weighing close to 300 pounds (136 kilograms). As he approached the door to investigate, it opened slightly and he caught a glimpse of guns.

Thinking quickly, he threw his enormous bulk at the door and, while holding it shut, yelled to his roommates. "Danger, guys! Terrorists!" he shouted.

Weight lifting coach Tuvia Sokolovsky was the first of the other Israelis to realize what was happening. His family had been wiped out by the Holocaust a few decades before. "Through the half-open door I saw a man with a black-painted face holding a weapon," he said later. "At that moment I knew I had to escape."

Sokolovsky screamed to his friends and bolted to a back window, where he smashed through the double-paned glass. The jagged shards sliced his skin. But he managed to fall to the ground outside, somersault

Coach Tuvia Sokolovsky (right) escaped to safety. His weight lifters (from left), Ze'ev Friedman, David Berger, and Yossef Romano, did not.

to absorb the shock, and run to safety as bullets whizzed by him.

Meanwhile, the masked men were able to get through the door by using the barrels of two of the AK-47s as levers. With great difficulty, four of them managed to subdue the powerful Gutfreund. Then they took all six men in the apartment hostage. The hostages were fencing coach Andrei Spitzer, weight lifting referee Yakov Springer, track and field coach Amitzur Shapira, marksmanship coach Kehat Shorr, and wrestling coach Moshe Weinberg, who lunged at the captors and was shot in the mouth. The terrorists bound all six Israelis at the wrists and ankles.

Next a terrorist grabbed the wounded Weinberg and ordered him to point out where the other Israeli athletes were sleeping. Weinberg reasoned that his best bet was to lead his captor to the weight lifters and wrestlers. With their strength and fighting ability, they had the best chance of overpowering the terrorists. He pointed out Apartment 3, where a few minutes later the Palestinians took the occupants by surprise. The new captives were weight lifters David Berger, Yossef Romano, and Ze'ev Friedman, and wrestlers Eliezer Halfin, Mark Slavin, and Gad Tsabari.

In the minutes that followed, the terrorists marched the men out onto the sidewalk, intending to take them to Apartment 1. In the process, however, Weinberg attacked one of the masked men in a valiant attempt to turn the tables. A Palestinian killed him with shots from his AK-47. During the fight Tsabari escaped by running down the steps and into a parking garage. The captors and remaining hostages entered Apartment 1, where Yossef Romano also made a heroic attempt to overpower the

Israeli victims of the Munich massacre were (top from left) Yossef Gutfreund, 40, Moshe Weinberg, 33, Yossef Romano, 32, David Berger, 28, Mark Slavin, 18, and Yakov Springer, 52; (bottom from left) Ze'ev Friedman, 28, Amitzur Shapira, 40, Eliezer Halfin, 24, Kehat Shorr, 53, and Andrei Spitzer, 27.

terrorists. He met the same fate as Weinberg. That left nine hostages alive and tightly bound in Apartment 1, along with their captors.

By this time, the section of the Olympic Village surrounding Building 31 was stirring to life in response to the sounds of the gunfire. A village guard called Munich's police chief, Manfred Schreiber, and told him what was happening. Schreiber ordered him to gather the rest of the guards. They should quickly lock the village gates so that no one could get in or out, he said. While waiting for the city police to arrive, the guards should keep anyone already inside the village away from Building 31.

One exception to that second order consisted of the emergency medical technicians who arrived in an ambulance a few minutes later. They quickly but carefully lifted Weinberg's limp body from the sidewalk and put

it in the vehicle. The siren blaring from the departing ambulance awakened everyone in the village who was still asleep at that moment—a little past 5:30 a.m.

Not long afterward, Schreiber, a muscular man in his 40s, arrived with a throng of policemen. They set up a command post as close to Connollystrasse as was safe to do. Schreiber soon discovered how unprepared the West German government had been for such an event. The Olympic Village had not been guarded well enough, he concluded. Moreover, though he had not been trained in anti-terrorist methods, he was now expected to neutralize a gang of foreign terrorists.

Munich police chief Manfred Schreiber spoke to reporters at the press center outside the Olympic Village.

While Schreiber fretted about what to do next, members of the press got wind of the crisis. Disguised as an Olympic official, AP veteran sports reporter Will Grimsley made it into the command post. But since he did not understand German, there was little information he could relay to his colleagues on the outside. The widely known and respected ABC sports anchor Jim McKay was unable to get inside the village. So he improvised. After getting as near to the crime scene as he could, McKay began his network's coverage of the crisis with these solemn words: "I'm Jim McKay speaking to you live at this moment from ABC headquarters just outside the Olympic Village in Munich, West Germany. The peace of what has been called the serene Olympics was shattered just before dawn this morning."

Other reporters and photographers converged on the Olympic Village in the hours that followed. AP sports reporter Karol Stonger sneaked inside by posing as an Olympic swimmer. She got as close as she could to Building 31. According to an AP report on the crisis coverage, "Stonger talked her way into the Puerto Rico team quarters—always off limits to a girl—and found a spot overlooking the Israeli team housing area. Once she hid under a bed as police came by, then popped back to her vantage point." A member of the Puerto Rican rifle team lent her a rifle telescope so she could better see the Israeli building. She was eventually discovered by the head of the Puerto Rican delegation, who made her leave.

Stonger's AP associate, Kurt Strumpf, tried to get through the village gate but was turned away. Undaunted, he walked around the area, calculating possible sightlines to Building 31. Finally he set up his camera on the balcony of a building facing the Olympic Village. At that point, he was still unsure exactly where the hostages and their captors were.

For all Strumpf knew, he might be in the line of fire if the terrorists, spooked by the police, started shooting at nearby buildings. But he had been in dangerous situations

"The peace of what has been called the serene Olympics was shattered just before dawn this morning."

Smoke billowed on a Gaza road in June 1967 as Kurt Strumpf photographed an Israeli soldier giving first aid to a journalist. The photographer was then treated for his own injuries.

before and had escaped death twice while trying to do his job. Five years earlier, in June 1967, he had been covering fighting between Israelis and Palestinians in the war-torn region of Gaza. According to an AP report, Strumpf "missed death or serious maiming by only 10 yards" when a booby trap mine exploded, killing an Israeli reporter and injuring others. A falling rock struck Strumpf in the head. "Strumpf managed to make a dramatic picture of the scene," the AP reported, "before Israeli authorities bundled him off to the rear for treatment. He was back in action the next day with a bandaged head and a bruised shoulder." The AP said Strumpf had nearly been killed 19 years earlier in the same area while working as a freelance photographer covering the 1948 Arab-Israeli war.

Strumpf had always managed to complete his assignments. And he fully intended to complete his present task—documenting the Munich hostage crisis as vividly and accurately as he could.

The youngest photographer on the scene that morning was 18-year-old Bill Temko. "My friend the track coach gave me a USA track suit," he later remembered. "And he said 'I think this will work, you can sort of fake your way into the Olympic Village' and for the first week of the Olympics that's precisely what I did." Then, in the hectic morning of September 5, Temko suddenly caught the break of his life. He later said that "all of the ABC sports people were congregated and saying 'How are we gonna do this? We can't even get into the Olympic Village.' And I sheepishly raised my hand and said 'I think I can get us into the Olympic Village.'"

Desperate to get inside, the ABC people agreed to Temko's plan. Sure enough, he and ABC cameraman John Wilcox got past the guards and made it into a dormitory facing Building 31. They were only 50 feet (15 m) away from the hostage takers. "Initially," Temko later recalled, "we could even see through the windows of the dormitory. You could see the hostages sitting on the couch and you could see that they were somehow tied up. Shortly

Photographers did the best they could to cover the hostage crisis from outside the Olympic Village.

[the terrorists] decided they would close the curtains." Covering the hostage crisis "was terrifying," he later said. "But I was a naive 18-year-old kid, so I'm not sure I had any comprehension of what I was getting myself into."

Early in the morning the terrorists had tossed two sheets of paper to a policeman outside. The typewritten letter identified the men as members of the group Black September. The letter demanded the release of 234 prisoners, mostly Palestinians held in Israeli jails. The prisoners were to be freed within hours, by 9:00 a.m. Then they were to be taken to an Arab country. Only then, the letter said, would the hostages be released.

Schreiber stared at the letter in disbelief. Although the terrorists were clearly serious, he realized, they were hopelessly naïve about how long it would take to implement such a demand. Even if the German and Israeli governments agreed to the demand, Schreiber thought, close to a full day, at the least, would be required.

Knowing there was no way to make the 9:00 a.m. deadline, senior German officials decided to negotiate with the terrorists. A little after 8:30 a.m., Schreiber; Walter Troeger, the ceremonial mayor of the Olympic Village; and Ahmed Damardash Touni, a member of the International Olympic Committee (IOC), went to Building 31. As they made their way up the sidewalk, a man in a ski mask appeared on a balcony outside the apartment and watched them approach.

From his vantage just outside the village, Kurt Strumpf saw what was occurring. He raised his camera and started snapping photos, one after another, of the masked Palestinian. One of the images became internationally famous. Other photographers took shots of the figure on the balcony, but Strumpf's was the one that proved to be iconic.

Schreiber and his companions met with one of the Palestinians, who had removed his mask. Wearing sunglasses and a white hat and speaking in fluent German, he identified himself as Issa. It later became known that his real name was Luttif Afif. He repeated the demand made earlier in writing.

Schreiber hoped to defuse the situation with a

A masked Palestinian, whose image would become world famous, peered over the balcony of the apartment where the Israeli captives were held.

counteroffer. That showed his lack of training in dealing with international terrorists. He offered Issa a lot of money if he would release the hostages. "This is not about money," Issa barked at him. "Talk of money is demeaning."

When it was clear that this approach was useless, Schreiber decided to stall for time. He managed to get Issa to agree to more meetings later in the day. For the meeting that began at 4:00 p.m., the police chief arrived at Apartment 1 with West Germany's interior minister, Hans-Dietrich Genscher.

Issa (in white hat, front) gestured to a fellow terrorist during negotiations with West German officials.

This time Issa threatened to kill all the hostages right away if his demand was not met. In an emotional voice, Genscher told him, "You know our history, you know what the Third Reich did to the Jews. ... You need to understand that that can't happen in Germany again."

HONORING THEIR MEMORY

A stone memorial and plaque in Munich Olympic Park commemorate the massacre victims.

Ever since 11 Israelis and one German were murdered at the Munich Olympics in 1972, people have tried to honor their memory. But creating memorials for them has not been easy. Part of the reason is that some people, especially some officials in the International Olympic Committee (IOC), were shocked and embarrassed by the Munich massacre. Some of them have even said in private that it would be best not to call attention to the incident by memorializing the victims. This attitude became clear in 2012 in the months before the London Olympic Games. The IOC received petitions calling for a moment of silence for the massacre victims during the opening ceremonies in London. But the IOC refused.

That won't be the case at the 2016 Summer Games in Brazil. The IOC plans to set aside an area in the Rio de Janeiro Olympic Village to commemorate the 1972 victims. A moment of reflection is planned for the Olympics' closing ceremony.

A memorial in Munich is also in the works. The IOC has contributed money for building a hall of remembrance near the site of the Munich Games. It will describe the main events of the tragedy and include profiles of the 11 Israelis and one German who died.

A small memorial honoring the victims is in Munich Olympic Park. Simple and dignified, it consists of a long gray stone balanced on a smaller upright stone block. The names of the victims are etched in the stone in Hebrew. A plaque in front bears an inscription in German. A small plaque in German and Hebrew at 31 Connollystrasse, where the Israeli team was housed, commemorates the victims and lists them by name.

The Israeli Olympic Committee honors the victims with a memorial ceremony every year at the Monument of the 11 in Tel Aviv. It also sponsors a memorial service during every Olympic Games. Israeli athletes visit the monument on the eve of their departure for the games.

A Palestinian terrorist looked out the window of the apartment where the Israelis were held captive. A West German police officer dressed as an athlete and armed with a machine gun stood one floor up.

Genscher offered to exchange himself for the Jewish athletes. Other German officials made the same offer, but Issa refused both of them.

Late in the afternoon, Issa grew tired of the many missed deadlines and made a new demand. He wanted the Germans to fly him, his men, and the hostages to Cairo, Egypt, where the negotiations could continue. If the demand wasn't met, he said, the hostages would be executed. The German authorities agreed to fly them all

Journalists and onlookers gathered outside the closed Olympic Village as the hostage crisis continued into the night.

in helicopters to an airfield on Munich's outskirts. From there, they promised, a commercial airliner would take them to Cairo.

The promise was a sham. The Germans were actually planning an ambush at the airfield in which the kidnappers would be killed or captured and the Israelis rescued. Once again, however, the German authorities showed how poorly prepared they were for a crisis of this kind. When the Palestinians and their

hostages landed at the airfield just after 10:30 p.m., only a few German snipers were in place. A fierce firefight ensued between poorly trained German snipers and the well-armed terrorists.

Finally, some German police in armored cars showed up, pitifully late. Now worried that his men would quickly be killed, Issa ordered them to execute the hostages. All nine Israelis—four in one helicopter and five in another—were killed by a combination of gunfire and a hand grenade. Five of the Palestinians, including Issa, were also killed.

Israeli flags draped the coffins of the Munich massacre victims. The body of weight lifter David Berger, a native of Ohio, was flown to the United States. The bodies of the other 10 victims were flown to Israel.

ABC's Jim McKay made the fateful announcement to a waiting world. "We've just gotten the final word," he said. "When I was a kid, my father used to say our greatest hopes and our worst fears are seldom realized. Our worst fears have been realized tonight. They have now said that there were 11 hostages. Two were killed in their rooms. … Nine others were killed at the airport tonight. They're all gone."

ChapterFour
INNOCENCE IN SPORTS ENDS

Most of the memorable images relating to the hostage crisis at the 1972 Munich Olympic Games are black-and-white photos. Thousands were taken during the almost 24 hours in which the awful incident unfolded. Of those pictures, about 20 have endured the test of time. They still form a shocking slide show of the most vivid moments of the crisis.

Most unforgettable of all is Kurt Strumpf's stunning picture of the figure on the balcony. That masked being with lifeless holes where eyes should have been went on to become a highly memorable and symbolic image. In fact, people across the world came to view it as representative of the inhuman barbarism of all terrorists. *Life* magazine called the man "a masked figure of doom."

Other photos of the Munich Olympics that people often see in books and documentaries, and on websites, show the negotiations between German authorities and the terrorists. Also well known are shots of German police standing atop Building 31. At one point, the authorities considered having the police climb down the face of the building and leap directly into Apartment 1. But that plan was rejected out of fear that the terrorists would kill the hostages the moment the first policeman appeared. Also seen quite frequently are AP photos of the damaged helicopters in which the nine Israeli captives met their deaths.

The photo of a man called "a masked figure of doom" is a chilling reminder that terrorism can strike anywhere and at any time.

Temko, now a lawyer in his early 60s, talked about the historic nature of the Munich hostage emergency in a 2012 radio interview. "This was a unique moment, I think, in terms of both news coverage and sports," he said. "It was before the Internet, obviously. It was before CNN. It was before ESPN. So it really was, I think, the first time that

Americans watched a news event like this unfolding in real time. It really was the end of innocence in sports."

According to this view, the principal means of covering leading sports and historical events today are very different from past methods. Modern recording devices, for instance, make photos shot by a handful of trained journalists seem less important to documenting important events. Hundreds of millions of people own cell phones. During a crisis they can shoot photos and videos instantly. Such images can be shown almost immediately by many 24-hour TV outlets. People also routinely post them on the Internet.

Coverage of protesters demanding that the Games be stopped was shown around the world. Activities were suspended for a short time, but the 1972 Olympics continued.

TRACKING DOWN THE MUNICH KILLERS

Officials allowed three terrorists to be flown to safety in exchange for the passengers and crew of a hijacked jet.

The three terrorists who survived the gunfight at the airfield in the late hours of September 5, 1972, were captured by German police. But they were freed soon after that when they were exchanged for the captured passengers and crew of a hijacked Lufthansa jet.

The terrorists' release prompted the Israelis to launch an effort code-named Operation Wrath of God. Israeli agents tracked down and killed two of the three freed Munich killers. The third terrorist, Jamal al-Gashey, remains at large and is believed to be hiding in Syria or North Africa.

Israeli agents also tracked down and killed dozens of others thought to be linked to the Olympic crisis. Among those targeted in Operation Wrath of God was Abu Daoud, who had publicly admitted to being the mastermind of the Olympic massacre. Israeli agents found him in a hotel in Warsaw, Poland, in 1981 and shot him 13 times. Incredibly, he survived. He died in Syria almost 30 years later of kidney disease, and right to the end he expressed no regrets for planning the brutal 1972 attack.

The way images of large-scale international events are recorded is not the only thing that has changed since the 1972 Munich massacre. The presentation of the Olympic Games was itself forever altered. The dream of the founders of the modern Olympic movement was that the games could be separated from global politics. It was hoped that whatever ill feelings existed among nations, they would be temporarily put aside during the games.

But the 1972 Munich tragedy showed that this would no longer be the case. "Now you have to think about security," said Israeli Olympic swimmer Avraham Melamed in a 2012 newspaper interview. Melamed was sleeping in the apartment between the two that were attacked, and he slipped out the back door to safety. "Now you have to think about terrorism. Now you have to plan for it. It comes at an enormous price. And this beautiful thing that's supposed to symbolize forgetting about politics, forgetting about war, for this period of time ... now it's contaminated. Now it's contaminated forever."

For the 2012 Summer Olympic Games held in London, Britain paid $1.6 billion in security costs alone. This is similar to what China spent for security for the Beijing Games in 2008 and Greece for the Athens Games in 2004. Sadly, AP reporter Robert Reid remarks, these worries and costs are "all the legacy of the Munich massacre." As recorded for posterity by a group of photographers, it was "a long-ago day that changed the Olympic Games forever."

The dream of the founders of the modern Olympic movement was that the games could be separated from global politics.

The Olympic flag and national flags flew at half staff during memorial services at Munich's Olympic Stadium in 1972. The massacre changed the Olympics forever.

Timeline

1931

Gretel Bergmann sets Germany's national record in women's high jump

1933

Nazi leader Adolf Hitler comes to power as Germany's chancellor

1947

The U.N. creates a Special Committee on Palestine, intended to find a peaceful solution to conflict between Jews and Arabs

1945

World War II ends with the defeat of Nazi Germany by the United States, Britain, and the other Allies; the United Nations is formed

1936

Nazi Germany hosts the Summer Olympics in the German capital, Berlin

1939

Hitler's army invades Poland, starting World War II

1948

On May 14 Israel declares that it is an independent nation; the Arab-Israeli War begins

Timeline

1952

Israel's first Olympic team competes in the Summer Games in Helsinki, Finland

1981

Abu Daoud, mastermind of the 1972 Munich massacre, is shot by Israeli agents in Warsaw, Poland, but manages to survive; he dies in 2010

2012

The organizers of the Summer Games in London, England, spend $1.6 billion on security, partly as a result of the terrorist incident in Munich in 1972

1971

The Palestinian militant group Black September is established; in November its members assassinate the Jordanian prime minister

1972

Eight members of Black September slip into the Olympic Village in Munich, Germany, seize Israeli athletes, and demand the release of jailed comrades; by the end of the ordeal, all 11 Israelis and one German police officer are dead

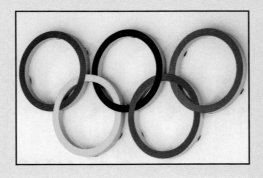

2015

Ground-breaking ceremony is held in Munich for a memorial to the massacre victims; another memorial is planned for the 2016 Summer Olympics in Rio de Janeiro

Glossary

anti-Semitic—discrimination against Jews because of their race, religion, or cultural background

crematorium—furnace in which dead bodies are burned

emigrate—to leave a home country to settle in another country permanently

firefight—an exchange of gunfire

iconic—widely viewed as capturing the meaning or spirit of something or someone

idyllic—peaceful and pleasant

journalist—person who gathers and reports news

proverbial—well-known

restitution—compensation for or restoration of something lost or stolen

telephoto lens—long-distance lens

Additional Resources

Further Reading

Burgan, Michael. *Terrorist Groups*.
Mankato, Minn.: Compass Point Books, 2010.

Friedman, Mark. *America's Struggle with Terrorism*.
New York: Children's Press, 2015.

Hay, Jeff, ed. *The Munich Olympics Massacre*.
Detroit: Greenhaven Press, 2014.

Skog, Jason. *The Legacy of the Holocaust*.
Mankato, Minn.: Compass Point Books, 2011.

Internet Sites

Use FactHound to find Internet sites related
to this book. All of the sites on FactHound
have been researched by our staff.

Here's all you do:
Visit *www.facthound.com*
Type in this code: 9780756552923

Critical Thinking Using the Common Core

During the Munich crisis, Kurt Strumpf and other photographers risked their lives to get photos of the terrorists. Why were they willing to go that far? (Key Ideas and Details)

When he heard about the crisis in the Olympic Village, AP reporter Will Grimsley did not have his press pass. He dressed as an Olympic official in order to get access to more information. Are journalists justified in using stealth to get an important story to the public? (Integration of Knowledge and Ideas)

The most famous photos taken during the crisis showed a man whose face was hidden by a ski mask, making him seem dehumanized. Why did that picture of a faceless person threatening innocent people come to exemplify the image of a modern terrorist? (Integration of Knowledge and Ideas)

Source Notes

Page 4, line 23: Will Grimsley, Associated Press Special Correspondent. "Commentary: Grimsley Recalls the Tragedy at Munich. *Los Angeles Times*. 19 July 1992. 28 July 2015. http://articles.latimes.com/1992-07-19/sports/sp-4670_1_munich-games

Page 5, line 1: Darrell Christian. "Thrills to Last a Lifetime." *Breaking News: How the Associated Press has Covered War, Peace, and Everything Else*. Associated Press reporters. New York: Princeton Architectural Press, 2007, p. 133.

Page 6, line 19: Robert H. Reid, The Associated Press. "1972 Olympics: Partying, pain in Munich." *The Orange County Register*. 21 Aug. 2013. 28 July 2015. http://www.ocregister.com/articles/olympic-353342-munich-german.html

Page 7, line 7: Ibid.

Page 9, col. 1, lines 7 & 13, col. 2, lines 8 & 13: "Commentary: Grimsley Recalls the Tragedy at Munich."

Page 25, col. 1, line 10, col. 2, lines 1, 6 & 11: "Munich Olympics Massacre: Officials Ignored Warnings of Terrorist Attack." Spiegel Online International. http://www.spiegel.de/international/germany/officials-ignored-warnings-of-munich-olympics-massacre-a-845867.html

Page 27, line 21: Cathi Knolinski. "Sportswriter for AP Karol Stonger is Kokomoan." *The Kokomo Tribune*. 5 April 1973, p.11.

Page 27, line 28: "Looking Back at the Munich Olympics." *The Madeleine Brand Show*. 89.3 KPCC. 6 Aug. 2012. 28 July 2015. http://scprv4-staging.scprdev.org/programs/madeleine-brand/2012/08/06/27732/looking-back-at-the-munich-olympics/

Page 32, line 18: Alexander Wolff with additional reporting by Don Yaeger. "When Terror Began." *Sports Illustrated*. 26 Aug. 2012. 28 July 2015. http://www.si.com/vault/2002/08/26/328187/when-the-terror-began-thirty-years-later-the-hostage-drama-that-left-11-israeli-olympians-dead-seems-even-more-chilling-and-offers-grim-reminders-to-todays-security-experts

Page 32, line 22: Simon Reeve. *One Day in September: The Full Story of the 1972 Munich Olympics Massacre and the Israeli Revenge Operation "Wrath of God."* New York: Arcade, 2006, p. 4.

Page 38, line 1: Michael Sokolove. "The Unexpected Anchor." *The New York Times*. 24 Dec. 2008. 28 July 2015. http://www.nytimes.com/2008/12/28/magazine/28mcKay-t.html?partner%3Drss%26emc%3Drss&_r=1&

Page 38, line 11: George A. Scott. "Clearfield Today-Tomorrow." *The Progress* (Clearfield, Pa.) 20 Sept. 1972, p. 4.

Page 39, lines 5 & 8 : "Mideast Coverage Difficult: AP Reports on Problems Encountered." *Denton Record-Chronicle* (Denton, Texas). 20 June 1967, p. 4.

Page 40, line 10: "Looking Back at the Munich Olympics."

Page 40, line 25: Ibid.

Page 43, line 3: Aaron J. Klein. *Striking Back: The 1972 Munich Olympics Massacre and Israel's Deadly Response*. New York: Random House, 2005, p. 51.

Page 44, line 3: Ibid, p. 52.

Page 49, line 2: "The Unexpected Anchor."

Page 50, line 14: Ben Cosgrove and Nilanjana Bhowmick "Terror at the Olympics: Munich, 1972." *Time*. 5 Aug. 5 2013. 27 July 2015. http://time.com/24489/munich-massacre-1972-olympics-photos/

Page 51, line 3: "Looking Back at the Munich Olympics."

Page 54, line 10: Kelly Whiteside. "Munich 1972: When terrorism 'contaminated' the Olympics." *USA Today*. 17 April 2012. 28 July 2015. http://usatoday30.usatoday.com/sports/olympics/story/2012-04-12/Munich-1972-When-terrorism-contaminated-the-Olympics/54325220/1

Page 54, line 25: "1972 Olympics: Partying, pain in Munich."

Select Bibliography

Bar-Zohar, Michael, and Eitan Haber. *Massacre in Munich: The Manhunt for the Killers Behind the 1972 Olympics Massacre.* Guilford, Conn.: Lyons Press, 2005.

Guttmann, Allen. *The Olympics: A History of the Modern Games.* Urbana: University of Illinois Press, 2002.

Hoffman, Bruce. *Anonymous Soldiers: The Struggle for Israel, 1917–1947.* New York: Alfred A. Knopf, 2015.

Klein, Aaron J. *Striking Back: The 1972 Munich Olympics Massacre and Israel's Deadly Response.* New York: Random House, 2005.

Large, David Clay. *Munich 1972: Tragedy, Terror, and Triumph at the Olympic Games.* Lanham, Md.: Rowman & Littlefield Publishers, 2012.

Large, David Clay. *Nazi Games: The Olympics of 1936.* New York: W.W. Norton, 2007.

Raab, David. *Terror in Black September: The First Eyewitness Account of the Infamous 1970 Hijackings.* Basingstoke, N.Y.: Palgrave Macmillan, 2007.

Reeve, Simon. *One Day in September: The Full Story of the 1972 Munich Olympics Massacre and the Israeli Revenge Operation "Wrath of God."* New York: Arcade, 2006.

Reporters of the Associated Press. *Breaking News: How the Associated Press has Covered War, Peace, and Everything Else.* New York: Princeton Architectural Press, 2007.

Schiller, Kay, and Christopher Young. *The 1972 Munich Olympics and the Making of Modern Germany.* Berkeley: University of California Press, 2010.

Index

About the Author

Historian and award-winning author Don Nardo has written many books for young people about modern history, including studies of the rise of Hitler and Nazism, World War II, terrorism, and many military topics. In addition, he specializes in ancient history and has published many volumes about the histories and cultures of the ancient world. Nardo, who also composes and arranges orchestral music, lives with his wife, Christine, in Massachusetts.